Reading Comprehension

Self-Monitoring Strategies to Develop Independent Readers

by Susan Mandel Glazer

S C H O L A S T I C
PROFESSIONAL**B**OOKS

NEW YORK • TORONTO • LONDON • AUCKLAND • SYDNEY

To my mother,
Mary Davis Mandel—
a special lady

Cover design by Vincent Ceci
Cover art by Beth Glick
Design by Jacqueline Swensen
Illustration by Mona Mark

ISBN 0-590-49136-9

12 11 10 9 8 7 6 5 4 3 2   2 3 4 5/9

Printed in the U.S.A.

Contents

Acknowledgments

I would like to express my thanks to Phyllis Fantauzzo and Denise Nugent, my colleagues, children, graduate students, and teachers at the Reading/Language Arts Clinic at Rider College, who continually try the strategies developed and modified in this and other written materials; Carol S. Brown and Camille Lombard Sanford, colleagues in the School of Education and Human Services, Rider College, and Lorraine L. Moreno, graduate assistant, for their helpful suggestions; Romy Celler, George Paul Olexis, Jason Wylie, and Larisa Deckert, the children whose creative products appear in the text; teachers Kathy Robbins of the Lawrenceville Public Schools and Valerie Corcoran of the West Windsor-Plainsboro Public Schools, both graduate students who provided some of the artwork and dialogue; the administration and the research and patent committee members at Rider College for granting me the time to complete this manuscript; my secretary, Gail Turner, for proofreading and professional loyalty in all of my activities; Terri Corvino, for her willing assistance; my delightfully intelligent editor, Terry Cooper, and talented associate editor, Liza Schafer, both of whose guidance made this project easy to create; some of my personal and professional friends— Morton Botel of the University of Pennsylvania, Eileen Burke of Trenton State College, Leslie Crawford of St. Cloud University, Gloria Fried of Georgian Court College, Bobbye and Gabe Goldstein, anthologists, Alma Quigley of Temple University, Lyndon Searfoss of Arizona State University; Jane Sullivan, Carol Satz, Estelle Brown, Judy Cohen, and all my NJRA friends, who continually provide support in all my endeavors; thanks to Kathy and Roger Hoff, the Maskantzes, the Swings, Judy, Jeff and Hank Glazer, for caring; thank you to my sister Lesley Morrow, whose research reinforces much of my work and Lynn Cohen, whose energy is inspiring, and my parents, Mary and Milton Mandel, who provided us with opportunities to read and write; to my husband, Richard Glazer, thank you for your never-ending support in all my professional endeavors. To others I know and respect, thank you for encouraging me to continue.

Introduction

Learning to read has been a major concern of parents, teachers, and children for centuries. For years, the teaching of reading focused on the mastery of skills. Teachers concentrated on *what* children learned, not *how* they learned (Sullivan, 1978). Individual skills were taught, with the expectation that children master them one at a time. It was believed that one skill depended upon another. A step ladder approach from the bottom up dominated instruction and learning.

In the past decade, educators and researchers (Smith, 1985; Goodman, 1986) have helped to redirect this type of instruction. Reading education today includes all literacy skills: reading, as well as writing, listening, and speaking. One does not learn to read in a static, linear manner, but in an interactive setting where people read and talk to each other about the text, write and discuss what has been read, and even discuss their written accounts of stories, information, and feelings. Instructional procedures resemble, in many ways, the "natural" language learning processes that occur when children learn to speak during the preschool years at home. The shift from a step-by-step skill-based program to a student-centered "holistic" view has caused educators to look at the relationships between how children read and write (the process) and what they produce (the product). Unlike in the past, the process is seen as being as important as or more important than the product. Children, teachers, and their interests are the center of learning rather than the materials.

In this book I have attempted to provide you with ideas for teaching children strategies that help them self-monitor their own comprehension as they read stories, content materials, poems, and songs. The strategies are designed to facilitate independent learning.

I have found that these strategies help children feel good about themselves as readers and writers. This occurs because they are provided with tools that permit them to have control over their learning.

This book is divided into three chapters. Chapter I defines comprehension and the variables involved in the process. Chapter II shares ways to create environments or settings that facilitate a desire for reading and writing independently. Chapter III includes strategies that guide children to self-monitor and make decisions about their reading abilities.

Through my years of experience working with children and teachers I have come to believe that all instructional strategies used in the classrooms must respect individual needs. All of us, children and adults alike, need to feel successful and confident in ourselves when we work and learn. Classroom environments can facilitate feelings of confidence when respect, sincerity, and control are shared among those who live and learn together in them.

I cherish the joy that I feel when I see children and teachers demonstrate personal satisfaction and feelings of success. That joy is the key to all learning, in and out of school.

What Is Comprehension?

Whaat is comprehension? What is understanding? How do we make sense of what we read and hear? Although these questions seem easy, their answers are complicated, for they involve thinking. How each of us thinks—how each solves problems—is what comprehension is all about. Comprehension occurs in all contexts. Each context, or the "text" of a given situation, has its own theme. We comprehend the text of a book when we read the print or look at the pictures. We also comprehend the text of a party, the text of a food market, and the texts of friends. We read these texts, or situations, and make meaning of the ideas they represent based on several variables: (1) previous knowledge that we have about each situation, (2) individual perceptions and feelings about each situation, and (3) our interests.

One way to explain texts of any sort and how each of us understands them is to think about a time that you've entered the text of a crowded room. The environment, which is the text you must understand, may be new for you. You know, however, some things about crowded rooms, for you've been in many. Sometimes they are business meetings, other times parties, and sometimes just many people waiting for a train or entry to a football stadium. Because people are dressed in festive clothing, you know from previous experiences that this crowded room must be a party. You walk in and stand for a while. Your perception of the situation makes you feel alone. You talk to yourself about what to do ("Maybe I won't know anyone here!"). Then you ask yourself, "Whom do I know in this room?" By asking the question, you've provided a direction for moving further into the text. You know, based on having done it before, that moving into the crowd permits you to "scan" the situation. Scanning allows you to sift out those faces you do know from those you don't. You search your memory, consciously or unconsciously, to find an old idea that helps you make sense of new notions resulting from things you see and sounds you hear in this new setting. Your eyes scan from left to right, and back again looking for something or someone familiar—a piece of furniture, a face; you listen for familiar sounds and voices.

As you review the crowd, your eye catches a man. Something about him causes you to stop. Your mind searches for a theme (text) that fits the man's characteristics. You try to "guess" who he is. You begin by making a picture in your mind while asking yourself questions about the man and what he might mean in different texts of your life. "Do I know him from work? Does he go to the same food market that I do? Is he a Cub Scout leader? Is he the father of one of my children's friends?" You answer each question by taking an "educated guess" based on your prior knowledge and experiences. You make a picture in you mind (an image) of the person in the food market, at a Cub Scout meeting, at work. Each image helps you to narrow possibilities in order to answer your questions. Suddenly, almost like magic, something happens. You get that "aha" feeling that says, "That's it! I know who this man is. I can picture him. He is my dentist."

How did you make sense of the text? What helped you to "read" the situation in order to comprehend this man in this setting? Skilled readers develop a series of strategies for helping themselves understand ideas. The example above demonstrates that they:

1. Use past experiences in order to notice familiar aspects of new settings (texts);

2. Use prior knowledge to figure out new situations;

3. Take risks and make "educated guesses";

4. Ask themselves questions and then search for the appropriate answers;

5. Scan the text for something familiar in order to connect something new with something in memory;

6. Review the text by going back (rereading);

7. Make comments to themselves about the text during reading;

8. Become personally involved with the text or situation.

Skilled readers use these and other strategies effortlessly and automatically. Readers interact with ideas, experiences, feelings, emotions, and concepts when they read. They are able to pull ideas from their memories and connect these appropriately to those in the text. They are able to do this for they are knowledgeable users of language and have learned how our language works. They know that:

1. Language has function and purpose;

2. Print can represent some ideas but not all;

3. Language has many parts;

4. Language is connected to thinking;

5. Language is a function of setting (language at home, for example, is sometimes different from language at school);

6. Reading, writing, listening, and speaking are used concurrently to communicate (Searfoss and Readance, 1989).

Readers understand that reading print is only one aspect of how humans communicate.

LANGUAGE HAS FUNCTION AND PURPOSE

Children learn to communicate before they come to school. Oral language is the major vehicle for communication. Even at very young ages, boys and girls learn language that helps them explain what they are feeling. They know that they can share events and explain and report ideas and situations with language. They also discover that language helps them negotiate in order to get what they want. Children use language for social and emotional survival. They cry when they are hungry, laugh when happy, and make sounds that provoke attention and love.

Written language is also used in early years for communication. Children write their own versions of words to send messages. **Figure 1-1** illustrates four-year-old Glenn's note to his grandmother describing the family summer vacation. As he wrote he said, "I went to the beach."

Figure 1-1

Reading, like oral language, is a social activity. Young children take great pride in demonstrating to adults that they can read the labels on favorite foods, traffic signs, their names, and the names of special people in their lives. In the years before school, they learn to recognize words in particular social contexts such as within the logo for their favorite fast food restaurant. The print acts as a picture, representing objects and activities. Reading aloud to children provides another social context that facilitates the development of a special bond between the person who reads, the child, and the stories themselves. You need to spend only a short time working with children to discover that they adopt their favorite phrases from stories and use them to create their own poems and narratives. One youngster I remember, who had heard many times:

Polly put the kettle on,
Polly put the kettle on,
Polly put the kettle on,
We'll all have tea,

said to his mother, while waiting to see his pediatrician:

Mommy put your coat on,
Mommy put your coat on,
Mommy put your coat on,
Let's go home.

Language also depends on cultural heritage and the importance and functions of the ideas expressed through language used in homes.

PRINT CAN REPRESENT SOME IDEAS BUT NOT ALL

Children know even before they learn to read that those little black squiggles on a page represent ideas, stories, and events. Observing a two-year-old talking while turning the pages of a book illustrates this concept. The roots of reading and writing are based on this early knowledge. Youngsters know about print because of their environments. At very young ages, many children can identify a milk carton by the words on it, a stop sign, a tube of toothpaste, and even their favorite candy bar by the printed letters. Children know what signs mean and that they represent something real—an object or an action. They learn, too, that the words representing concrete ideas usually don't express feelings. They discover that often one word represents more than one idea. Think about the following sign (or a similar one), which is often posted outside a restaurant:

SHIRTS AND SHOES ARE REQUIRED TO ENTER THIS ESTABLISHMENT.

The literal interpretation of the words could mean that shirts must go into the establishment. Shoes must, too. Although this sounds absurd, we, as skilled readers, understand the message even though the author of this text has not used printed language clearly to represent the ideas. We know the special idiosyncrasies that our language imposes and can interpret the text in spite of them. New readers and those who learn to read in a language other than their native tongue have a difficult time doing this. Phrases like "good grief" and "terribly good" have different meanings depending upon their contexts. Multiple meanings cause confusion. How strange, for example, that the word "good" should be coupled with the word "grief" to represent surprise or astonishment.

I have often thought that the task of making meaning from text is like the task of a detective (see **Figure 1-2**). Readers and detectives have similar problems. Each is faced with events (or words). Each must search for clues or information. As pieces of information are uncovered, some are discarded, and some saved. The more the detective searches, the more he finds. For the reader, each piece of information alters the meaning of a text.

Figure 1-2

The comprehension process is complex. Our language is partially responsible for the complexities. Each person's previous knowledge and experiences compound the process. The prior knowledge and past experiences "owned" by humans cause the print to represent different ideas to each. An author's writing skills play an important part in comprehension, too. Some authors write in such a way that meaning is not clear. An unclear text forces its readers to spend much time searching in order to solve the meaning problem.

LANGUAGE HAS MANY PARTS

Language is complex not only because it bears different messages to each of us, but also because the language system has several components: (1) the print, (2) the rules that permit us to create sentences, and (3) the meanings of words, sentences, paragraphs, and longer units.

1. Print represents sounds. Children are expected to take clues from the print and make the sounds that are represented by these squiggles. Many children learn the names of letters, the alphabet, and the sounds letters represent before they come to school. The print (graphics) and the sounds (phonemes) form the graphophonic cue system of language. Children must comprehend this system in order to read.

2. Our language also has a set of man-made rules. These rules govern sentence structure. These rules are learned naturally as children communicate with adults and siblings. Children learn, for example, how a sentence begins and ends. They know, because of a special ability that is possessed only by humans, how to change sentences, add to them, delete things from them, and condense them. We know intuitively whether a sentence is really that. "The ice cream is good," is a sentence. When we see, "Ice cream good the is," we know that the words are arranged in such a way that they cannot possibly be a sentence. Young children generalize sentence-making rules they've learned, sometimes inappropriately. The sentence, "Stephanie goed home," for example, was probably created because the child has heard the "ed" participle representing the past tense in other contexts. She has generalized the use of the rule, for she has not yet learned the word "went." Language rules are learned from birth by all children regardless of their native language, and for the most part this learning happens, amazingly, without formal instruction.

3. Meanings of words, sentences, and longer units of print are referred to as semantic cues. Children learn to understand words by listening. They learn to use language by talking with adults and siblings long before they come to school. Children make meaning of language based on responses during these early interactions. The meanings of print are assigned during reading by each reader based on his knowledge of language. Each of us carries around summaries of experiences in our memories, and each relies heavily on these in order to make meaning of print. Children learn to understand print based on their knowledge of words and how these words are used in different contexts. Learning word meanings and how to use them in different situations is complex and often confusing. Children are often expected to use one word in several contexts, adjusting the meaning of the word to fit each context. One teacher said to a child who was disruptive, "For the present time, just sit quietly in the cafeteria." The child, when asked after two hours by the school cook why he was there, replied, "My teacher told me she would give me a present if I sat here."

LANGUAGE IS CONNECTED TO THINKING

All of us have a collection of ideas stored in our memories. These ideas are grouped together almost like files in a cabinet. The human memory has an enormous amount of storage space. The more files of information the reader stores in memory, the more probable her ability to understand print. These accumulations of information collected from experiences in the world are applied to new information, and meaning occurs. When readers have little or no information about the contexts they read, they struggle to make meaning. **Figure 1-3** illustrates how impossible it can be to understand a text when there is little information stored. The word "present" described in the anecdote above represented a gift to the child but "time" for the teacher. Individual interpretations of text often result in comprehension problems when reading in school.

Reading and writing, all literacy skills, are dependent upon a complex system of variables. Children must read a lot and be read to. They must talk to adults and other children. They need to write and draw pictures about what they hear and see. Most important, they must create language by talking, writing, and discussing their compositions. All language—written, spoken, heard, or read—

Figure 1-3

involves thinking. As Lindfors (1987) suggests, language permits children to make ideas real, to make them into things. It allows them to shape and act on ideas, much like they might mold clay. The connection between language and thought requires that children participate in all sorts of language activities to comprehend effectively.

LANGUAGE IS A FUNCTION OF THE EXPECTATIONS OF THE SETTING

The way we learn language differs from setting to setting. In early language acquisition at home, children say words, frequently mispronouncing them as they attempt to move the muscles in their mouth to make the sounds. Often these words are difficult to understand, but body language—pointing, gesturing, showing—helps the listener to understand the mispronounced words and phrases. Adults may applaud these mispronunciations as appropriate attempts to use language during the learning process. Similarly, in school settings, children may invent spellings as they learn that writing communicates ideas. Invented spellings are similar to attempts at saying words when learning to talk. Mispronounced words and scribbles both represent words and ideas. Scribbles and invented spellings tell adults that children know how to create written text, and that they are aware that it is a code used to convey meaning.

Language learning in school, however, is often different than at home. The trial and error experimental language learning activities that occur naturally at home are sometimes missing in schools. Often there are correct and incorrect, appropriate and inappropriate ways to say and write words. Spellings, in many school settings, must be correct. Format—the placement of words on paper, letter formation—is sometimes expected to appear like typeset print. On playgrounds, slang or dialectal pronunciations of words are appropriate modes of behavior. In school, however, they are not. Differences in the purposes and functions and in the expectations for the production of language pose problems for children. The confusion can create barriers that stop children from reading and writing. The audience who will read children's writing, and who will listen to children talk, must always be primary in the minds of adults who provide instruction for children.

READING, WRITING, LISTENING, AND SPEAKING ARE USED CONCURRENTLY TO COMMUNICATE

Reading, writing, listening, and speaking are all integral parts of the comprehension process. In order for spoken language to be purposeful and functional, there must be someone to listen to it. In order for reading to happen, a writer must create the text. Children know this before they come to school. When a child brings a book to an adult, crawls into his lap, and says, "Read it to me," she is sharing this knowledge. When a three-year-old writes and talks at the same time, he demonstrates that creating the print and creating the oral text are integrated behaviors.

Language is developmental. The abilities grow as the child grows. Language skills are part of the physical, intellectual, emotional, and social development of children. Such growth is an interactive, integrated process that involves all aspects of human behavior. Comprehension depends on this holistic development in environments where healthy interactions are ongoing, where children and teacher feel happy about learning.

JOURNAL ACTIVITIES

Now that you have read this chapter, you might want to try the following activities. They have been designed to help you better understand the processes children engage in as they attempt to comprehend.

1. Find a notebook for yourself and begin to keep a daily journal. In that journal, write what you remember about how you learned to read. Then write your feelings about the experiences.

2. Fold a page in your journal so that there is a left and right column. In the left column, write about a situation that has been difficult for you to understand. Then, in the right column, write your feelings about the situation and your reasons for not understanding.

3. Take yourself and your journal to a playground or mall where children play. Watch them play for at least twenty minutes. How many actions do you notice that are related to the development of reading, writing, listening, and speaking—the literacy skills? When do you see language used functionally? Write these in your journal.

CHAPTER 2

Environments That Facilitate the Development of Comprehension

S uccessful comprehension in all academic subject matter depends upon well-organized, well-managed, and well-planned lessons and routines. In my work I have learned that children and teachers need to make joint decisions so that all feel ownership (control) of ideas and materials. It is the teacher's job, however, to create a print lab (Searfoss and Readance, 1989)—that is, a classroom filled with purposeful print that facilitates language learning. The print lab classroom can be designed to encourage learners to take risks, make decisions, and know about themselves and how they function with print.

I have found that classrooms that feel safe, warm, and sincere instill in children a desire to read and write. Trust seems to emanate from the teacher to each child, and from one child to another. Most interesting are children's perceptions of themselves—their feelings about their abilities to read and write in a secure environment. When I feel good about what I am doing with learners, they seem to feel good, too. I recall a time when a child who had just written a composition asked, "Do you like my story?" Her need for adult approval seemed to indicate lack of confidence in her own production. My response, "How do you feel about it?," was worded to encourage independent thoughts and decisions about her story. The child shrugged her shoulders, and said, "I don't know." I responded, "Then I guess I don't know either." The youngster seemed a bit perplexed and walked back to her work space. She turned back to me before reaching her desk, however, and said, "I guess I really do like my story." I responded, "I am glad that you like your story. I like it too!"

I, and others, have found that children's perceptions of themselves as learners have a powerful impact on their desire and abilities to learn to read and write (Corcoran, 1991; Gordon, 1990; Glazer, 1991; Lipson, 1983). My years of experience with children in classrooms and the research cited above support the influence of nurturing environments on children's positive perceptions about learning. We need to guide children to explore and experiment with reading and writing. Freedom to explore their feelings and ideas through the materials made available and the consistency of classroom routines and activities are all-powerful elements that influence children's impressions of reading and writing. Children need to be interested in and familiar with materials. This motivates learning. The more successful children are with reading and writing, the happier they will be about such activities. The more conducive the environment, the more learning will occur (Morrow, 1985).

Literacy-rich environments focus on functional and purposeful activities that guide and foster children to:

1. Take risks while learning;

2. Make decisions about learning;

3. Self-assess how and what they learn;

4. Learn to think about ideas and write independently.

I have developed a checklist to act as the starting point for creating a print-rich environment (**Figure 2-1**). Consider your own classroom as you review the list. All items on the checklist are discussed later in this chapter.

Features of a Print-Rich Environment	Comments
The classroom is "print-rich." Print plays a functional role.	
The classroom has its own library, including published books and student-authored books.	
The environment fosters risk-taking.	
Children self-monitor their ability to read by using self-selection strategies.	
Models of good reading behavior are provided.	
Time is allotted for independent silent reading and writing.	
The environment provides opportunities for sharing and responding to reading and writing.	
Oral reading is purposeful and voluntary.	
The room has cozy, small places for individual reading and writing activities, and larger spaces for group work.	

Figure 2-1

PREPARING A PRINT-RICH CLASSROOM

I recall the time that our family took a car trip in the fall season to see the changing colors of the leaves. My sisters, ages two and four, and I, age six, asked to stop to use the "girls' room." At the service station, the three of us quickly realized that there were two bathrooms. I knew that one was for girls and the other for boys. I ran back to the car and asked, "Mom, what letter does 'girls' begin with?" Her answer permitted me to find the lavatory labeled with what I thought was the word "girls." The word begin with the letter "g." We entered the lavatory, but quickly discovered that this bathroom was unlike any other we had seen before. There were no doors or seats for us. I ran out to my parents and asked, "How do you spell 'girls'?" After my mother spelled the word, I recall saying the letters over and over again in my head as I dashed back to meet my sisters. The word "girl" was not on the label on the door. Only the first letter ("g") matched the word our mother spelled. We then shouted "Mommy, come here." Our mother's laughter helped us realize that the word she'd spelled did not match the word on the door, and we were in the bathroom for "gentlemen." I learned, at that young age, that print was functional.

Functional print is just what the name implies; it serves a function. Labels on bathroom doors, signs communicating directions or information such as "Library Corner" or "Put papers here," and schedules of daily events and activities all serve real purposes. Directions for collecting snack money and for carrying out assignments, such as "Water the plants every Monday and Thursday," or "Feed the fish a pinch of fish food every day at 10:00, " are all functional activities that can be "printed" for children to read. Like my younger sisters and myself, all children need to read in order to carry out functions.

Consider how much functional print you are using in your classroom. Teachers I have known have asked themselves several key questions as they reflect on their use of functional print. These questions are presented in **Figure 2-2** so that you will be able to ask them of yourself.

Uses of Functional Print	Comments
Are the laboratories, classroom library, and other important places labeled?	
Are there appointment charts for the children to schedule meetings with me and other children?	
Are written instructions provided whenever possible?	
Are there mailboxes to encourage writing notes and letters to one another?	
Do I write stories myself and display both the drafts and the finished products?	
Have I created a publishing center which includes: ■ paper of several sizes and colors, lined and unlined ■ pencils, pens, markers, crayons, and chalk ■ different examples of writing to encourage composing: poems, short stories, jokes, riddles, newspaper headlines, story starters (Once upon a time—, In the middle of the night—, One hot afternoon in July—, etc.) ■ bookmaking supplies ■ one or more word processors ■ one or more typewriters ■ lists of words children frequently want to write ■ word books: dictionaries, alphabet books, a thesaurus, books with rhymes, etc.	

Figure 2-2

THE CLASSROOM LIBRARY

Many educators and researchers (Arbuthnot and Sutherland, 1977; Beckman, 1972; Cullinan, 1989) have stressed the importance of providing children with daily opportunities to experience literature pleasurably, and of incorporating literature in social studies, science, and math activities. A classroom library center entices children into books and encourages reading (Morrow, 1985; Morrow and Weinstein, 1986). We know that children in classrooms that include literature and other book collections read fifty percent more often that children in classrooms without such collections (Bissett, 1969). Classroom libraries that are comfortable have the following features:

1. A rug to sit on;
2. Some soft pillows to lean on while reading or listening to others read;
3. A soft, cuddly, oversize chair for a child to cozy into and read;
4. Shelving no higher than children's eye level for self-selecting books;
5. Approximately five books for each child in the classroom;
6. Display shelving for magazines, newspapers, and important books;
7. Sign-out charts for taking books from the library;
8. A book-drop box for returning books.

Figure 2-3 shows the floor plan of a classroom that effectively incorporates a library center.

Choosing Books for Your Library: Matching Children and Books

Books interesting to children facilitate comprehension and motivate learning. Books that motivate five- through eight-year-olds include the following:

Books without words: texts in which pictures tell the story;

Picture concept books: texts in which pictures are labeled;

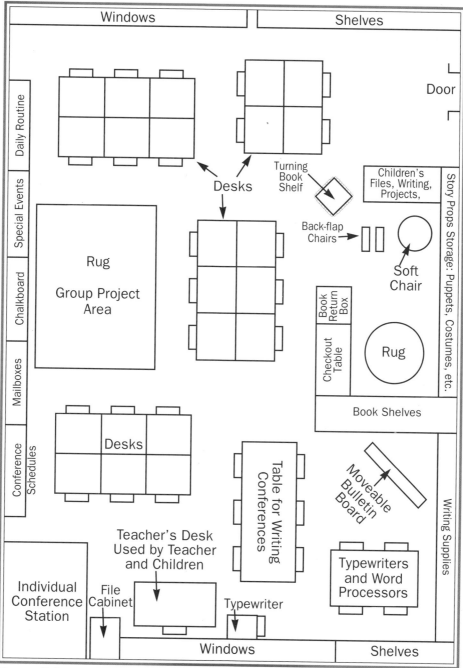

Windows

Shelves

Door

Daily Routine

Special Events

Chalkboard

Mailboxes

Conference Schedules

Desks

Turning Book Shelf

Desks

Children's Files, Writing, Projects,

Back-flap Chairs

Soft Chair

Rug

Group Project Area

Book Return Box

Checkout Table

Rug

Book Shelves

Story Props Storage: Puppets, Costumes, etc.

Desks

Table for Writing Conferences

Moveable Bulletin Board

Teacher's Desk Used by Teacher and Children

Typewriters and Word Processors

Individual Conference Station

File Cabinet

Typewriter

Writing Supplies

Windows

Shelves

Figure 2-3

Picture story books: texts in which pictures tell the story;

Traditional literature: fairy tales, fables, myths, and folktales;

Easy-to-read books: texts with few words, words and sentence patterns that are repeated, familiar concepts for the age level, and predictable plots and language patterns;

Content books: nonfiction texts about holidays, foreign countries, famous people, different cultures, historical events, etc.;

Books of poems: anthologies focusing on specific themes;

Riddle and joke books: texts based on word play;

Reference materials: encyclopedias, books of facts, and how-to books;

Periodicals: children's magazines and newspapers, as well as daily newspapers.

Some materials can be part of the classroom library's permanent collection. Others, including periodicals and books children need in order to do work in their content studies, will vary throughout the school year.

It is important to make sure that classroom book collections reflect children's current interests. Interests differ at each age and at each stage of development. **Figure 2-4** outlines the interests of "younger readers" (children age five to seven) and "older readers" (children age seven to nine); it also includes a list of titles that accommodate these interests.

Interests and concerns of children in their preteen years include fiction and nonfiction: short stories, novels, books on specific topics, fact books, how-to books, encyclopedias, newspapers, and periodicals. Reference materials available for research and other projects should include dictionaries, thesauruses, spelling checkers, instructional materials (how to write a paper, how to do research, etc.). Preteens enjoy books with multiple meanings, figurative language, idiosyncratic language, and stories with complex plots and multiple episodes. These "in-betweeners" concern themselves with issues identified in **Figure 2-5.**

READING INTERESTS

Interests	Example
YOUNG READERS — 5 TO 7	
■ Interested in self	*Dandelion*
■ Simple plots	*Where's Spot?*
■ Cumulative plot structure	*The House That Jack Built*
■ Repetitive language	*The Very Hungry Caterpillar*
■ Fantasy	*The Tale of Peter Rabbit*
■ Like to be surprised	*Just Like Everyone Else*
■ Like to see the "good" win in the end	*Sam, Bangs and Moonshine*
OLDER READERS — 7 TO 9	
■ Interested in knowing that they are like others	*Today Was a Terrible Day*
■ Like some books that are easy to read (limited vocabulary)	*Mooch the Messy*
■ Enjoy realistic situations	*Ramona and Her Father*
■ Can sometimes deal with multiple meanings	*Charlotte's Web*
■ Enjoy identifying with the main character	*Ferdinand*
■ Like chapter books	*Valentine Rosy*

Figure 2-4

(Cullinan, 1989)

READING INTERESTS	
Interests	**Example**
PRETEENS — 9 TO 12	
■ Personal and social aspects of life	*Bridges To Cross*
■ Parental relationships	*Dinky Hocker Shoots Smack*
■ Peer relationships	*Homecoming*
■ Sports	*Hoops*
■ Mystery and suspense	*Dragons in the Water*
■ Adventure	*The Truth Trap*
■ Dealing with illness and handicaps	*Go Ask Alice*
■ Death	*Friends Till the End*
■ Love and romance	*When We First Met*
■ History and historical content in fiction	*The Fighting Ground*
■ Alternatives to reality	*The Magical Adventures of Pretty Pearl*
■ Humor	*The Adventures of Huckleberry Finn*
■ Ethnic heroes	*The Autobiography of Miss Jane Pitman*
■ Coming of age	*A Day No Pigs Would Die*
■ Fantasy	*The Lion, the Witch, and the Wardrobe*
■ Music	*I Will Call It Georgie's Blues*
■ Problems in life	*The Pig-Out Blues*

Figure 2-5

(Reed, 1988)

THE RISK-TAKING ENVIRONMENT

Benji, age seven, stopped me in the school hall one afternoon and asked, "Susan what do you do here?" Attempting to help him take a risk and make an educated guess at the same time, I responded by redirecting his question. "Benji," I responded, "what do you think I do here?" "I think," said Benji with a most serious look on his face, "I think that you're the principal." "That's a pretty good guess," I remarked. "But why do you think that?" I asked further, seeking justification for his risk-taking response. "Well," he began, "I think you're the principal because you just walk around being nice to everyone and you don't do very much."

Benji took a risk. He made an "educated guess" about my role in the school's environment. He felt comfortable with me and with the environment in order to make that guess. Making an "educated guess" about what texts mean is an important part of comprehension. Guessing is risky for all of us, teachers and children. Often errors are made when one "guesses" the answer to specific questions. Errors, however, are essential for learning.

What permits risk-taking to occur? **Figure 2-6** identifies the essential characteristics of a risk-free environment. It is a place where children trust their teacher and other children, where confidence is built, and where collegiality unites all who become part of the classroom. Think about your classroom. Is it an environment in which children are free to take risks? Is risk-taking seen as an important part of learning?

ORAL READING

Can you recall a time when you were expected to read in front of a group? Before you read, your fingers tingled, your hands became clammy, your heart began to beat quickly. This is the way many children feel about reading orally to peers. I recall when ten-year-old Eddy was asked by his classmates to read his composition to the class. Eddy's gestures seemed to indicate that he felt hesitant. When the class president spoke out and said, "Eddy, first-graders read their

Characteristics of a Risk-Free Environment	Comments
Children read orally when they want to. Sometimes planned purposeful oral reading occurs—scenes from plays, parts of favorite books. Rehearsal time is provided before children read out loud. This rehearsal is a MUST. Children read aloud ONLY if they agree to.	
Children select books for recreational reading and for information. Sometimes—like an old friend—they select the same book again and again. Other times they select books that are too difficult. This helps some children feel better about themselves in relation to their peers.	
Children's invented spellings are accepted. Children are encouraged to view writing as a tool for getting their ideas on paper. All writing in any form during first drafts of compositions is accepted because this encourages children to write.	
The teacher shares what she writes. This provides children with a model for sharing among themselves. The teacher understands, however, that some children may not want to have their stories read aloud.	

Figure 2-6

Desired behaviors are learned when children see teachers model those behaviors. Therefore, the teacher reads and writes when the children read and write.	
The teacher uses direct praise to tell children what she likes about their work. Evaluative or punitive comments (e.g., "You can do better than that if you try") are avoided. The goal is to help children build internal feelings of satisfaction from personal growth.	
Instructional strategies are used to develop independent readers and writers (see Chapter III).	
Teachers help children know their limits. Class rules are made WITH the children. The rules are consistent and followed by all.	

Figure 2-6

stories to us," it was impossible for Eddy to refuse. Eddy wrote well, he read well, and he worked well independently. Performing in front of a group was not one of his favorite activities. As he approached the front of the classroom he began to cough. His coughing became so vigorous that he had to stop reading. Reading out loud was difficult, actually impossible for Eddy. Reading out loud was unnatural and uncomfortable for Eddy.

Some children adore reading to their peers; others do not. Some love to read to adults. Others however, prefer to read to themselves. Creating situations in which children have the option to select times to read to others may help those, like Eddy, who find this activity difficult. When oral reading is purposeful and meaningful, it may invite a reluctant reader to become involved. Some activities that may entice children to read orally include (1) reading a part in a play, (2) being the daily story reader, after rehearsing the oral reading several times in school or at home, and (3) sharing self-authored books. *Oral reading is appropriate when children feel a purpose for sharing, and also when the teacher and children agree, in advance, that this will occur.* Not all children will be comfortable reading out loud. Those who find it difficult may develop a dislike for reading in general if oral reading is required. You can observe your children as they read out loud and decide with each if oral reading is important or appropriate.

SELF-MONITORING STRATEGIES FOR GUIDING CHILDREN TO SELECT BOOKS FOR RECREATIONAL AND INFORMATIONAL READING

My experiences have helped me learn that a child's desire to read is the single most important variable for successful reading. Children have a desire to read when they select their own books. Selecting books is a form of control. It also promotes responsibility for learning. Twelve-year-old Kyle once said to me, "I don't like this book." My response was, "Well, you selected it. You need to make a decision. Let's talk about why you don't like the book. Then you can select a book that includes things that make you want to read it."

I have found that children select books appropriate for reading when (1) books in which children are able to recognize most of the words are available, and (2) books that interest them are available.

Recognizing words is an easy task to self-monitor. The "fist-full-of-words" rule and directions for using this rule described by Glazer and Searfoss (1988) are based on the concept developed by Jeannette Veatch. Say to the student: "Hold up your hand with all of your fingers straight up. Now you may select any book. Begin with one page. Read it to yourself. Each time you do not know a word, put a finger down. If all of your fingers go down on that page, you have a fist. Try to read three more pages. If you make a fist for all of the

pages, the book is too difficult. Try another."

Often children will select the same book again and again. This is a form of rehearsal. Frequent contact with words increases vocabulary, as well as comprehension. Like good friends, familiar books with familiar words make children feel good about themselves as they read.

Some children select books that are too difficult. This often happens because children may feel the need:

- to be like peers;

- to read what an older sibling reads;

- to be read to;

- to feel better about themselves because their school reading ability, age, and grade levels don't match.

INVENTED SPELLING

Learning to spell is a developmental process. It resembles the development of oral language. When toddlers begin to speak, words are mispronounced. Often these mispronunciations resemble the words that youngsters attempt to say. The more children speak, the better pronunciation becomes. The more they write, the more they are able to spell words correctly. Beginning writers spell words the way they sound. This permits them to focus on getting their ideas on paper. I stress to children, however, that it is important to spell correctly when they share their writing with others. A desire to share inspires young writers to edit their writing, which includes correcting spelling errors.

MODELING BEHAVIOR: DO WHAT I DO

Modeling behavior is probably the most powerful instructional procedure in classrooms. We demonstrate good table manners, ethics, morals, and values by carrying them out. We teach religious customs, too, by engaging ourselves and children in these simultaneously. Learning about comprehension is best accomplished when children have a model for behavior. If we want children to love reading, we must do as we want them to do—read and love to read.

Don Holdaway (1986) has outlined a "commonsense" four-step learning process appropriate for literacy learning. His steps include (1) observation of modeled behavior; (2) partial participation by the learner with coaching from the model (teacher); (3) role-playing or rehearsal in the absence of the model; and (4) performance, where the child shifts roles and does the modeling for the teacher. If applied to a reading situation, the following might occur:

STEP 1: Observation

Teacher reads a book to herself. She does this every day during the time the children are working or reading on their own.

STEP 2: Partial Participation

Some children sit in chairs near the teacher and, as they listen, help to complete repeated sentences, rhyming words, and familiar phrases. The teacher guides children to say words as if part of a chorus. At times, the teacher points to phrases and words in the text.

STEP 3: Role-playing

Multiple copies of the book that was read are in the class library. Some children get the book during free time and attempt to read it. Some read it; others pretend to read the words, and retell the story. There is sufficient free time available for these rehearsals and role-playing times to happen naturally.

STEP 4: Performance

Child says, "Listen to me read," and adult does; child asks to read to a group of children or reads to a doll or another child.

Holdaway's four-part model permits children to observe, become partially involved with, rehearse, and then perform literacy activities. This model facilitates a desire—almost a burning need—to perfect skills. It forces each of us to rehearse the skills. The hard work creates ownership and feelings of control over situations. The desire to learn also creates for many a strong need to share accomplishments.

DIRECT PRAISE

Jennifer, a quiet nine-year-old, chose to write a story about her new baby brother. She began several times, each time erasing the paper until she had created a hole in it. Each time she began, I watched this tedious process—her ritualistic behavior that seemed to help her get ready to write. My heart ached each time she began, and I wanted very badly to help Jennifer begin the story. I knew, however, that I had to let her do it herself if she were to become independent. After ten minutes, I could no longer stand watching her go through this painful experience. Just as I was about to step in and provide help, though, Jennifer wrote for five minutes without stopping. I noticed when she stopped and immediately went over to her table and said, "Jennifer, I watched you begin that story, and write and write and write and write and write until just this minute. I am so happy that you were able to begin the story and write for such a long time." Jennifer beamed with joy, and immediately went to the cabinet for another piece of writing paper. She began another story immediately, this time without erasing or crumpling the paper.

Praise helps all of us feel more competent and better able to take risks. Most often praise comes in the form of evaluation. I have used phrases such as "Very good," "That's great," and "Wonderful," when children have performed school tasks meeting certain expectations. Although these terms are positive, they are also vague. They tell nothing about the behaviors children have carried out.

Test grades and report cards are the most commonly used form of evaluation. If performance is high, these can be helpful for creating a desire for further learning. Low grades, however, can have a negative effect on learning. Grades are as vague as the phrases above. They tell the child very little about what was accomplished.

I have found that direct praise provides specifics, encourages further learning, and makes the child aware of the things he does that help his learning occur. To follow are a few examples of direct praise:

- "I feel very good about the way you read your book on your own."

- "Using the fist-full-of-words rule, like you did, makes you independent. You don't need the teacher's help to choose a book."

- "I am glad you noticed your mistake and found a way to change it."

I have found, after thirty years of teaching, that punitive remarks or negative praise such as, "Johnny, tell Michael that word" or "Jane needs to pay attention," causes feelings of inadequacy and embarrassment. Poor test scores and grades on report cards cause these feelings as well. Testing and report cards with grades are a fact of life in schools. It is for these reasons that I find it vitally important to use direct praise to encourage children—especially those whose grades hover at the lower end of the scale—to feel good about themselves and their reading and writing.

CHILDREN KNOW THEIR LIMITS

As I reflect on my teaching experiences—from children to in-service teachers—I realize how important consistency is for learning. The more consistent I am with materials, my language, and my routines, the more effective I am as a teacher. I have found that charts that guide children's weekly and daily activities and personal contracts between each child and the teacher are important "limit-setting" devices that help develop independent readers and writers. They permit children to monitor and manage their classroom routines. **Figure 2-7** represents a daily schedule. You may want to use this as a guide for developing your own daily routines. The large blocks of time for literacy activities permit flexibility for meeting individual and small groups of children.

In my teaching, I plan individual conferences to meet specific needs during the language arts time block. You may want to create a daily or weekly conference schedule so that consulting time is available for individual or small groups of children (**Figure 2-8**). Modifications of the daily schedule might be necessary in order to accommodate other school activities.

Daily Schedule for Grades K-6

8:30–8:55 Opening Activities

Announcements; classroom business; individual activities:
selecting books from the classroom library, independent reading,
and independent writing

9:00–11:40 Language Arts

Read and discuss stories; read and retell in groups; read and retell
individually; guided and unguided reading and writing activities; literature
and content materials; peer work: sharing compositions, research projects
in content areas, editing, writing, creating plays, etc.; individual reading
and writing: journals, letters, response to reading; storytelling: story time,
puppet plays, making books; mini-lessons

11:45–12:35 Lunch

12:40–1:20 Exercise

Monday:	Tuesday:	Wednesday:	Thursday:	Friday:
Physical education	Outdoor activity	Physical education	Outdoor activity	Special

1:25–1:40 Story Time

Storytelling; book sharing time

1:45–2:20 Math

Group and individual activities

2:25–3:00 Social Studies and Science

Group and individual activities that include writing, reading,
and research activities

3:05–3:15 Review of Daily Activities

Group or individual

Figure 2-7

(Adapted from Routman, 1991)

| | | | | | | | | | | | | | | | | | | | |

Comprehension Conference Schedule (sample)		
Time	**Monday**	**Tuesday**
9:00–9:20	*Kevin: Oral retelling, Nate the Great— Chapter 1*	*Mary Ann: Self-monitoring retelling, Cinderella*
9:30–9:50	*Melissa: Self-monitoring conference (first one), Tammy and the Giant Fish*	*Jonathan: Writing conference, second draft of creative story*
10:00–10:20	*Free*	*Brian, D.J., Stephanie, Ross, Sarah, Kathy: Written retelling in response to story*
10:30–10:50	*Free*	↓
11:00–11:20	*Free*	*Kevin: Oral retelling, Nate the Great— Chapter 2*

Figure 2-8

Comprehension Conference Schedule

Wednesday	Thursday	Friday
John, Ted: Instruction (prompts) for story problem, Choose Your Own Adventure Series *Use guided retelling checklist ↓	John, G.P., Eddie, Lance, Buzz: Instruction—Self-selection practice, fist-full-of-words rule	Stephanie: Retelling Ramona
	Free	John: Retelling Charlotte's Web *Focus on episodes
Free	G.P.: Instruction— Using self-monitoring sheet as a guide for writing	Free
Eddie: Tape and book reading with assistance, The Very Hungry Caterpillar	Brian: Instruction— Self-monitoring a computer retelling, Charlotte's Web	Free
Wendy and Pam: They are writing a play and want to know "how to do it"	Buzz: Oral, unguided retelling onto tape, Mooch the Messy	Jamie: Rehearse storytelling— Oral reading by choice

Figure 2-8   Note that free spaces permit flexibility in scheduling unexpected conferences.

SUMMARY

Children's ability to learn to read and write is dependent on environments that are risk-free, consistent, and conducive to meeting individual needs. Such environments are designed to accommodate children who find it easiest to learn by sitting still as well as those children who are inclined to squirm as they write or fidget while they read. Literacy-rich environments are packed full of materials that satisfy children's curiosities and will entice them to read and write.

Self-management devices, self-selecting materials, and joint decision-making activities increase children's ability and desire to monitor their own growth and needs. Direct praise encourages independent learning and healthy attitudes toward risk-taking.

JOURNAL ACTIVITIES

The following activities have been designed to provide you with more information about environments that facilitate comprehension. As you carry them out, you will be an active observer and learner. Most important is reflecting on your observations as you reread your journal and asking yourself, "Am I creating a classroom that is a warm and secure environment for me and my children?"

1. Walk around your classroom. Make a list of all of the print-rich variables that entice children to read and write.

2. Make a list of all of the times you use writing in functional ways both at home and at school.

3. Write down all of the activities that could be used to foster purposeful reading and writing in your classroom.

4. Do children have a purpose when they read orally? Ask children when they read aloud, "Why are you doing this?"

5. Write down all of the times that children should be able to self-select books for recreational and informational reading.

6. Identify your children's interests. What do you do to help your children select books that reflect their interests?

7. Write down your feelings about invented spelling. Talk to colleagues about this concept and compare their feelings to yours.

8. Try to explain the rationale for accepting invented spelling to parents. Write this explanation in your journal. Read it through several times and rewrite the explanation until you feel confident sharing the ideas with parents.

9. List times that you feel you will be able to use direct praise. After you use the praise, write down each child's reaction to this form of praise. List times that you might be able to use direct praise again.

10. Each time you catch yourself using punitive language to reward (or reprimand) a child, write it down. Reflect upon your words, and then think about forms of direct praise that might have been used instead. Write these in your journal.

11. List all of the activities you model and can model for children.

CHAPTER 3

Becoming an Independent Reader

*Strategies That Guide Children
To Self-Monitor Their
Reading Comprehension*

I n this chapter I describe several of my favorite strategies for teaching comprehension. The strategies have been developed with one very important goal in mind: to help children learn to self-monitor their own comprehension. They encourage students to take risks, make decisions, exercise responsibility, and exert control over their own activities. I have found that these comprehension strategies encourage most children ages six through sixteen to read and respond to their reading independently. The strategies are divided into three categories—those used before reading, after reading, and during reading.

BEFORE-READING STRATEGIES

I have found, and so have others, that it is important for children to know something about a book before they read it. Having information about the content improves comprehension. It is important to make children aware that they can understand what they read best if:

- they know something about the book before they begin to read it;
- they know enough about it to predict what it will be about.

The teachers I have worked with recommend that children use the following strategy:

1. Look at the book's front and back covers and title page;
2. Look at the pictures and read a paragraph or two to get a feeling for the language of the book;
3. Think about what you've observed;
4. Predict what the book will be about.

Use the words "look," "think," and "predict" whenever you are discussing comprehension. Hang the words in appropriate places in the classroom. "Look" might be placed near a new library book or by a window. "Think" could be represented by a caricature of a bright-eyed child thinking about something special. Try to use the words informally in conversations as often as possible. I might say, for example, when a child looks out of the window, "Are you looking and thinking about what you see out there? What can you predict about the weather by looking at the clouds?" Encourage children to attempt to draw reasonable conclusions (**Figure 3-1**).

I have found that it is important to have children look, think, and then make predictions about many things. You might ask them to predict what the auditorium program will be like, what the lunch menu will be, how they will feel at an upcoming party. When possible, ask your students to justify their predictions. When a child predicts, for example, that someone will be out sick, you could ask, "What makes you think that?" A response

Figure 3-1

like "He's been coughing all morning" justifies the prediction. You can easily model the prediction strategy for the children. Place an easel or chalkboard with the surface divided in half with a vertical line near the lesson site. Title the left column "Predictions" and the right "Why." Before reading, hold the book up so children can see the cover. Then say, "I am looking at the pictures and thinking. I am asking myself, 'What can I predict about this story from the cover?'" Answer your questions and write responses in the left-hand column as you talk. Then say, "I made that prediction because . . . ," and write the justification for your response in the right column next to the prediction. Continue by saying to the children, "What predictions can you make?" As children volunteer, write predictions exactly as they are said. After each response ask, "Why did you make that prediction?" Write the response in the right column. Show the back cover of the book; then ask for predictions and justifications and write them down. Once you feel that you and the children have had sufficient time to predict, read the story to the children. Say to them before you read, "Listen carefully as I read to you, to see if your prediction was correct." Some children may want to read by themselves to determine whether their predictions were correct.

I have found this activity to be most successful when it is carried out twice weekly, over several weeks. Repeating the activity helps children learn how to look, think, and then predict independently. They learn the language and the procedures, thus moving toward the ultimate goal—independence in reading.

Once children understand the "look, think, predict" strategy, further reinforcement can be encouraged by using the "ideas before reading" sheet (**Figure 3-2**). First, model using the sheet by hanging an easel-size version in your teaching area. Tell the children that the sheet is similar to the one you used together, but that they can use this one on their own. Say, "On this sheet of paper write your own predictions about the story you choose to read. In the 'Why' column, write your reasons for your predictions. You do not need to be concerned with spelling, handwriting, punctuation, or anything except the predictions and your reasons. After you read your story, see how closely your predictions match the story."

IDEAS BEFORE READING (sample)

My Name: __Kylie__

Date: __Oct 14__

Book: __Cinderella__

Author: __E. Lecain did the pictures__

My Prediction	<u>Why</u> Did I Make That Prediction?
I think the book is about a girl who is pore.	Because on her picture she has a ragy dress.
I predict she gets rich.	Because inside the book she is in a fanzy dress.
I predict shes really a princes.	Ther is a princes in it.
I think I am going to like it.	I don't know!

Figure 3-2

You and your children need to decide how often to use the prediction sheet. I recommend that the sheet become a "natural" part of reading. That means that some children would use it each time they selected a story, and some would not. The sheets can be kept in the writing or library corner so children feel free to take one as needed.

AFTER-READING STRATEGIES

After children finish reading their books, they can use the "ideas after reading" sheet (**Figure 3-3**) to help them compare their predictions with what actually happened in their stories. Prepare a folder or portfolio for each child, into which they can file all of their comprehension activities. These portfolio collections help you and each child systematically review their productions. Children begin to notice what they are able to do and what they need to work on. The materials, or data, in these portfolios can provide the basis for sharing children's progress with their parents.

I have found three additional types of "after-reading activities" successful for increasing comprehension and determining each child's strengths and needs. These are (1) unguided retellings, (2) guided retellings, and (3) self-monitoring strategies.

Unguided Retellings

Unguided retellings are often spontaneous, voluntary dialogues and discussions about books. Children love to share what they've read. They will share with you, a classmate, and other eager audiences. I recall nine-year-old Michael, who read an entire series of books. The series *Choose Your Own Adventure* by Edward Packard, excited him so much that he felt he had to tell me about each adventure not only after he completed a book but also after reading each chapter. Michael would run up to me in the school cafeteria and say, "Mrs. Glazer, guess what! I predicted how the story would end in the middle of the book." Michael would tell me the stories, and I remained attentive until he ended his retellings. Talking about reading is retelling. I believe that allowing children to retell stories to

IDEAS AFTER READING (sample)

Name: Kylie   Date: Oct 14

Book: Cinderella

Author: E. Lecain did the picturs

The book was about: Cinderella who is pore and her stepmother is mean and her sisters to. But she got marryed to a prins and was happy.

Predictions that were correct: She was a princes. She got rich. I liked it. It was abowt a pore girl.

My feelings about the book: I like the book and my mom used to read it when I was 3 but it was diferent.

Figure 3-3

an attentive audience is probably the most powerful way to facilitate their desire to read. The retelling also demonstrates children's comprehension to themselves and adults.

Children and adults have been "retelling" what they've read for centuries. This powerful tool, retelling immediately after reading, is a natural, unguided approach that demonstrates what children recall from books. The unguided retelling strategy has many advantages. It:

- is easy to prepare;
- is suitable for developing a range of language abilities;
- is flexible in its use;
- requires a minimum of teacher involvement;
- provides practice for many literacy skills, including reading, and writing as well as organizing information, recalling it, and reacting to it (Brown and Cambourne, 1987).

Unguided retellings can also be more formal, scheduled activities. Conferences can be planned by you or each child. One ten-minute conference weekly for each child in your classroom can provide sufficient information about comprehension. Unguided retellings, spontaneous or planned, are wonderful for determining what children need to know to improve comprehension. Some children prefer to retell their stories orally. Others may prefer to write them. I have found that it is important to encourage each child to retell in the way that is most comfortable for her.

Some children need to be guided to retell stories. I have found that the easiest way for me to teach this to children is in either a large or small group procedure. I say to the group, "I will read the story (name the title and author). When I finish reading, take a piece of paper (or a tape recorder), go back to your tables, and retell the story as if you were telling it to a friend who has never heard it before." Immediately after reading the story, I repeat the instructions: "Retell the story as if you were telling it to a friend who has never heard it before." Some children will retell best when they write. Others may find that handwriting is difficult and it inhibits their ability to share information. For these children, retelling orally and recording the retelling onto audio tape at the same time is an option. A written retelling is a product of comprehension. A transcript of the oral retelling on tape is also a product of comprehension. The following written retelling of *Gregory the Terrible Eater* by Mitchell Sharmat was composed by eight-year-old Romy independently (**Figure 3-4**). A

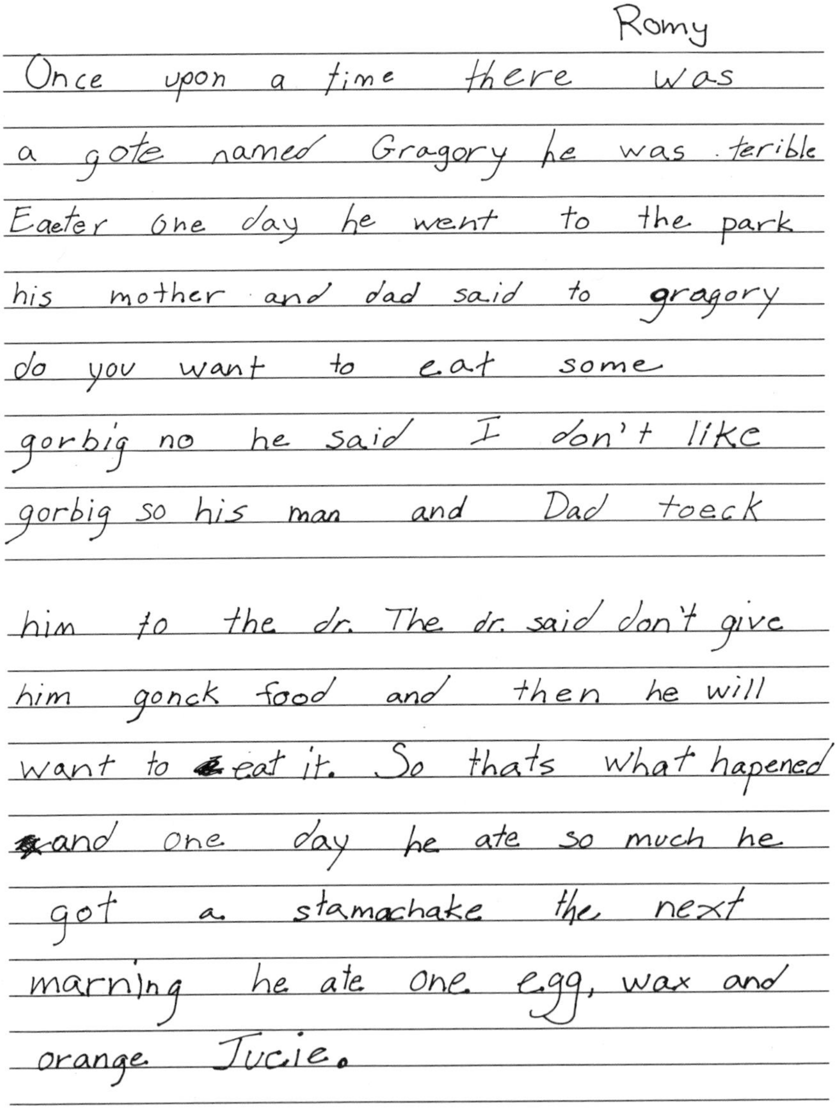

Romy

Once upon a time there was a gote named Gragory he was terible Eaeter One day he went to the park his mother and dad said to gragory do you want to eat some gorbig no he said I don't like gorbig so his man and Dad toeck

him to the dr. The dr. said don't give him gonck food and then he will want to eat it. So thats what hapened and one day he ate so much he got a stamachake the next marning he ate one egg, wax and orange Jucie.

Figure 3-4

transcript of an unguided oral retelling will be shared in the self-monitoring section of this chapter.

I believe that it is important, each time you ask children to retell, to use the same words. The repetition helps them to remember the rules, providing them with the security they need to retell independently.

Guided Retellings

Guided Retellings are designed to direct children's responses when retelling. Guides, referred to as "prompts," are specific questions that are used during retellings to help those children who need encouragement to recall after reading. We guide children to hold a fork correctly when they are unable to use the utensil effectively. When small hands have difficulty opening a milk carton, we intervene just in the nick of time to avoid frustration. Children need prompting when they are having difficulty beginning a retelling or continuing one.

Imagine that you have just completed a book. You know that you are expected to retell the story immediately as if you are telling it to a friend who has never heard it before. An individual retelling conference is scheduled to occur at the conference table and is listed on the daily calendar. The decision to hold a conference was a joint one; you have participated in several unguided retellings before. Even though you know you are about to retell it, you discover that you are recalling only parts of the story. You decide to use the same prompts your teacher used earlier. These might help you remember more.

The prompts for guiding retellings of stories are included in **Figure 3-5**. These prompts, or questions, should be used again and again for each story. Children internalize the questions, and after several prompted retellings, begin to self-monitor retellings by questioning themselves. I have found that self-questioning is a strategy that helps children become independent readers.

During guided retelling, I sit next to the child. I ask the child to begin the retelling. I say, "Retell the story (or chapter) to me as if I have not read it before. As the child retells, I give the appropriate prompt *only* when the child hesitates. The following is a transcript of

GUIDED RETELLINGS

Story Elements	Prompts/Questions
INTRODUCTION	Once upon a time . . . It happened this way . . . It all began . . .
SETTING *Place* *Time*	Where did the story take place? When did the story take place?
THEME *Main character* *Other characters*	Who is the story about? Who else is in the story?
PLOT *Problem or goal*	What is the main character's problem (or goal)?
EPISODES *Events*	What happened first? What happened next? (Use this prompt for each episode in the story, if necessary. Some children will need only one prompt to recall events.)
RESOLUTION *Problem solver*	How was the problem solved? or How did the main character achieve the goal?

Figure 3-5

an oral guided retelling session carried out by Valerie, Romy's teacher. Romy self-selected the book *Mice at Bat* by Kelly Oechsli. Her reluctance to begin and carry through a retelling on her own persuaded the teacher to use prompts throughout to guide Romy to retell successfully.

Teacher: When did the story take place?

Romy: At midnight.

Teacher: Where did the story take place?

Romy: In the park.

Teacher: Can you tell me more details about the setting? Where it took place and when it took place?

Romy: After people leave the park of baseball, the mice come in and clean up the park of baseball and then they always come in and play baseball.

Teacher: O.K. And who is the main character?

Romy: Kevin.

Teacher: Kevin's the main character. Who are the other characters?

Romy: Young Willie, Joey, and other mice.

Teacher: And what is the problem? What happens in the story?

Romy: There's a baseball game at twelve sharp and the Boomers and another team. There's a cat that comes in and gives a letter that they'll be playing and there was a cat that was in it and he was the pitcher and there was a rat in the game and he made a home run and Young Willie got hurt by the rat and at the end of the story the other team went down with Young Willie.

Teacher: Tell me the problem again?

Romy: It was how to let Young Willie win.

Teacher: What other story details do you recall?

Romy: None. It was only about a baseball game.

Teacher: Now, that retelling was great. Now, try to retell it without me using prompt questions.

Romy: O.K. There were some mice that lived in a park and there were some boys that always played in the park. After the boys would go home, they would clean up the park and they would play some baseball. One day a cat came and brought a letter that said there would be a baseball game at twelve sharp. And the Boomers and another team would play too. And other people came to the baseball game on Saturday night. There was a cat that was their pitcher and there was a rat that was a batter and the rat was on the Boomer's team and the cat and they were very happy because their team won.

Reporting children's success is best done in narrative form. Romy's parents might like to know that this guided retelling demonstrates that Romy was able to read the book independently and recall the main character and five or six of the other characters. She remembered all three episodes and the plot as well. Romy ended the story appropriately. It was interesting to notice that once Romy was prompted to recall, she was able to retell the story, and that she did so even more completely the second time without prompts. The second, unguided retelling demonstrates Romy's sense of story. The prompts probably helped Romy gain confidence and "get started" so that she was able to carry out the unguided retelling. It was evident from both retellings that Romy needs guidance for understanding story problems or goals and how these are resolved. The following illustrates one teacher's approach to this aspect of reading comprehension:

Teacher: Do you know the story of Cinderella?

Romy: Yes. She wanted to go to a ball, but she didn't have a dress for the ball.

Teacher: That's right. She had a problem. The problem was that she did not have a dress. Romy, can you think of another problem Cinderella had?

Romy: Yep. Well, she had this horrible stepmother who was mean. And she said that she had to do all of the work and then she could go to the ball. But there was so much work.

Teacher: So Cinderella had two problems. The first was that she did not have a dress for the ball. The second was that she had to do all of her work before she could go to the ball.

Romy: And she needed shoes, too.

Teacher: So, what did Cinderella do to solve her problems?

Romy: Well, she got her fairy godmother to get her the dress and glass shoes, and also she made a pumpkin into a carriage, and she made horses with mice.

Teacher: Now, tell me again. What was Cinderella's main problem?

Romy: She wanted to go to the ball but she needed a dress and she needed to get her work done.

Teacher: Right! And how did Cinderella solve the problem?

Romy: With her fairy godmother.

Teacher: Great! Now, tell me the problem in *Mice at Bat*. Let's look for it in the book, together.

Self-Monitoring Strategies

Self-monitoring strategies are those that children use on their own. In order to self-monitor, however, children must be provided with specific activities to respond to stories and guide their thinking. I recommend three activities to develop self-monitoring skills: (A) literary response journal, (B) creating questions about books, and (C) self-monitoring conferences. I have found that children learn self-monitoring most successfully if it is modeled.

A. Literary Response Journals

A literary response journal is a diary or log that some children keep to record their responses to readings. I have found that when I respond daily to my own reading by writing in my literary journal in the classroom, children watch. Some develop the desire to write their own responses to reading by observing the modeled behavior. The journal provides them with a chance to use writing as a tool for communicating.

B. Creating Questions About Books

Young children, even before they come to school, ask questions about everything. They ask why the grass is green, why grandmother is making Thanksgiving dinner, and why you don't read that story again. Children's natural curiosities create the need to question. I believe that this natural curiosity can be used to help improve children's comprehension. Children might ask their questions orally or in writing. Children's questions permit teachers and children to discover:

- aspects of the story that are important to each child;
- the type of information each selects to remember.

Creating questions can be an individual or paired activity. I suggest that children write questions individually as part of their journal activities. Questions can be written before they retell in their journal. The journal entry (**Figure 3-6**) illustrates a twelve-year-old's retelling and self-questioning after reading Sheila Greenwald's *All the Way to Wits' End*. When he wrote this entry he was just beginning to feel confident enough to carry out the activity without asking for guidance from his teacher.

Some children may feel more comfortable creating questions with a partner when they read the same story. After each child writes two or three questions, they take turns asking each other the questions. Peer review is part of the process, and children begin to learn from one another.

C. Self-Monitoring Conferences

Self-monitoring conferences are carried out using an unguided written retelling or a transcript of an oral retelling. I have developed a guide sheet (**Figure 3-7**) as an organizational tool to help children review and assess their own comprehension. After using this guide with many children, I am convinced that it is a successful tool for both self-monitoring and developing a sense of story structure. What they learn through self-monitoring is later reflected in their own stories.

PROCEDURE

Imagine that you and a child are sitting next to each other at a conference table. You have transcribed the child's unguided oral retelling of a story. Romy's unguided oral retelling after listening illustrates an example of such a transcription (see page 59).

The transcript was prepared the evening after the child retold the story onto a cassette tape. Begin the conference with:

ALL THE WAY To WITS' END

* (Predictions)
I think this book will be about
a family that is moveing and they got
lost.

(Chator One) (Retell)

This story is about a girl
named. Drucilla that is a twelve
year-old and she has move with her
family to a contony from Loves
Landing. (It is raining) She is home sick and she
just want's to go home but her new
house is to small and she and her mom can't get
her mom to get ride of the old-
handed-down cloths, funiture But if
she got ride of them she could get
new everthing.

Main Idea
The man idea is she want new cloths

and want's to go home.
Questions
1. If she going to get home how is she
going to get home?
2. What sason are they in?
3. How old a her brother and
sister?

Figure 3-6

SELF-MONITORING RETELLING GUIDE SHEET

Story Elements	Yes	No	
I included an introduction.			
I included the setting:			
where the story takes place;			
when the story takes place.			
I included the name of the main character.			
I included other characters.			
I included the problem (or goal).			
I included the story episodes.			
I told how the problem was solved.			

Next time I need to remember _____

_____

_____

Name: _____

Title of story: _____

Author: _____ Date: _____

Figure 3-7

- the transcript on the table;
- the book on which the retelling transcript is based;
- the self-monitoring guide sheet in front of the student (**Figure 3-7**);
- several pencils with erasers.

The following transcript and dialogue of Romy's unguided oral retelling of *Big Al* by Andrew Clements illustrates how the conference might proceed:

> *Once upon a time there was a big fish that had no friends and he looked very scary, but he was very nice. And all the little fish didn't like him, so he tried to disguise himself. One day he turned colors and he followed the little school of fish. Then he was so clumsy that he bumped right into them and before he could say, "Excuse me," the little fish were gone.*
>
> *One day the little fish were talking with Big Al. He was so happy and then he got some sand in his throat and then he started to sneeze and then all the fish ran away and then after, a few minutes later, the little fish had something all around them. It was a big net. The fishermen were trying to get them. So Big Al charged and he bit into their net and then he let all the fish free. But when all the fish went out, Big Al got stuck. And then the fishermen started to pull him up. But then they took a look at him and they didn't like him so then they throw him back in the water and then all the little fish were his friends and those fish would have friends like Big Al.*

Teacher: Romy, I listened to your retelling tape of *Big Al* by Andrew Clements. I have typed it. Let's read it together.

(The child and teacher read the transcript together, chorally. This helps the child to read all of the words she has spoken on the tape.)

Teacher: Now, let's see what you remember after reading the story.

Look at the retelling checksheet. Read the first line with me. (If the child has difficulty keeping her place, as Romy did, the teacher might place a ruler under the first line, and together they read, "I included an introduction").

Romy: Yes, I did that.

Teacher: Show it to me in the transcript.

Romy: Here it is.

Teacher: Read it.

Romy: "Once upon a time there was a big fish that had no friends and he looked very scary, but he was very nice."

Teacher: Yes, you included an introduction, and that was "Once upon a time." I really like the way you found that and read it. Check the box that says "Yes." Now, did you tell where the story took place?

Romy: Um-m-m (child reads out loud to herself) u-m-m. I don't know.

Teacher: Well, let's read and see.

(Both reread the story to themselves to find out if the location is mentioned.)

Romy: I don't think I told where.

Teacher: I agree with you. That's really great that you know that you didn't include the place where the story happened.

I have found this type of dialogue to be invaluable for guiding children to self-monitor, review, and assess their comprehension. It also teaches story structure, since the child is expected to justify responses by locating the elements of a story in the transcript or written retelling. This type of self-assessment helps the child determine not only what she knows but also what she needs to learn. Children like Romy have a handle on learning and feel they are in control. A secure environment that fosters risk-taking—trial and error—facilitates self-assessment.

I have also learned from watching children in self-monitoring activities that they discover that the elements used by authors can also be used by them to write their own stories. I remember when eight-year-old John ran up to me and excitedly shouted, "Mrs. Glazer, Mrs. Glazer, you know what? I put my retelling checksheet on the computer and used it to write a story. I asked myself the questions, and just wrote the answers, and up popped my story, just like that!" With the guidance described above, and practice, children will find out for themselves, as did John, that they can use the retelling sheet to determine if they have included all elements of stories in their writing.

DURING-READING STRATEGIES

I have found that when I read something difficult to understand, I often stop during my reading and ask myself, "What does that mean?" Stopping during reading and asking questions is one strategy to help understand the text. If you think about it, you will probably be able to recall many times when you've talked to yourself about your reading. Good readers do this almost all the time. Some good readers are aware of their behaviors, and others do it spontaneously. I have asked many children if they know what good readers do to help themselves understand difficult reading materials. We have learned from children that some are able to explain what they do to read successfully, while others cannot (Corcoran, 1991; Winograd and Greenlee, 1986). The following responses from three children, ages eight, nine, and ten, reveal the children's thoughts about good reading behavior, particularly their own.

Eight-year-old G.P. defines reading as paying attention. (See **Figure 3-8.**) It is presumed from his responses that he is in a reading group, where children sit together in a circle. G.P. perceives part of good reading as looking at the teacher. This is his way of saying, "I know that I need to attend."

Nine-year-old Jason's response, "be quiet, be good," is similar to G.P.'s. (**See Figure 3-9.**) He, too, understands and perceives reading as attending to a teacher-controlled task. Both children consider themselves good readers part of the time. Their ambiguous responses indicate that taking a risk is difficult and may be dangerous.

Name some things good readers do when they read.

tha loke at you

Name some things poor readers do when they read.

thae loke at the ceiling

What kind of reader are you?

sum people are better but I am gad

Your name: _G.P._
Your age: _8_

Figure 3-8

Name some things good readers do when they read.

be quiet
be good

Name some things poor readers do when they read.

talk
run a round

What kind of reader are you?

a good reader.
a quiet reader.

Your name: _Jason_
Your age: _9_

Figure 3-9

Name some things good readers do when they read.

I think good readers picture that they are in the story or book so they can remember things better from the book

Name some things poor readers do when they read.

Poor readers just look at the words and don't think what they mean.

What kind of reader are you?

I think I'm a good reader because I can picture I'm in the story and I can remember what happened.

Your name: *Laura*
Your age: 10

Figure 3-10

Ten-year-old Laura knows that to understand one must "act upon" the words or pictures by making connections between what is in the text and what is in one's mind. (See **Figure 3-10**.) Laura does this by making pictures in her mind about the text. Poor readers, according to her, identify or recognize words but don't think about what they mean. Meaning to poor readers is secondary, or unimportant.

The strategies shared in this section are those often used by good readers naturally and automatically. Educators have found that teaching these strategies to all readers helps them understand how to interact and respond to text effectively (Bird, 1980; Palincsar and Brown, 1984; Brown and Lytle, 1988). Children learn to think about what they read when teachers model the behavior and then provide the opportunity for children to rehearse the good reader strategies independently and with peers. The goal for all readers is to make these strategies a habit.

Thinking aloud during reading is referred to by Farr (1990) as a "thinkalong." Readers can think along as they read, using prior experiences and perceptions of the ideas to create meaning. Several educators have developed strategies for guiding children to think about text on their own (Eddy and Gould, 1990; Wilson and Russavage, 1989; Russavage and Arick, 1988). The before-reading strategies mentioned earlier, and those that follow, are designed to encourage children to act upon the text. The reader thinks along and attempts to look into ideas in his mind during reading. I have used the following list of thinkalong strategies with even the youngest children:

1. Making a picture in one's mind about the text;
2. Predicting from pictures, subtitles, and words during reading;
3. Asking oneself questions about the text;
4. Going back and rereading when the text doesn't make sense;
5. Personalizing the text based on one's own experiences;
6. Guessing the meanings of words during reading.

Modeling these strategies helps children learn how to use them. Imagine that you are getting ready to read a story to a group of children. So that there is a picture in your mind about the story, let's suppose that you are going to read one of the many versions of the fairy tale *Cinderella*. Your intention for reading is to model how one thinks along in order to understand the text during reading. Using many of the strategies in one session is a good way to model the concept of thinking along. It is best, however, to use only one strategy at a time for instructional purposes. Continued use of a strategy, once a day for two weeks, will guide children to use it for themselves. A special story-reading time provides the most conducive setting for such instruction. The following procedures are adapted from the works of several individuals (Eddy and Gould, 1990; Farr, 1990; Wilson and Russavage, 1989; Russavage and Arick, 1988).

Modeling Thinkalongs: Procedure 1

Hold the book in front of the children. Put your finger to your forehead indicating that you are using your brain to think. (See **Figure 3-11**.) You need not tell the children with words what you are doing. They will learn quickly that the words you are saying when

Figure 3-11

your finger is at your temple are your thoughts and not the author's words.

Begin by saying, "I wonder what this book is about?" (asking yourself a question). You read the title and then make comments: "This is a name of a person" (predicting from the word). "The picture tells me that this girl, whose name is probably Cinderella, is poor. I can tell because her clothes are made of rags, and my mom uses rags to dust (personalizing and making a prediction based on prior knowledge). She is looking at a castle on top of a hill. I bet that this is about a poor girl who wants to live in the castle" (predicting from picture). Continue this in front of the children and then begin to read the book.

As you read the story stop and say, as you put your finger to your temple, "I am thinking that _____ ." You should be sharing ideas that come into your mind about the story. Do this when:

- you are able to predict what will come next;

- you are not sure about an idea so you ask yourself a question;

- you are not sure of an idea so you reread to clarify the information (or sometimes to answer your question);

- you can demonstrate unfamiliarity with a word's meaning by rereading the text to help you make meaning of it;

- you can personalize an idea in the story by relating it to something in your life.

1. Making a Picture in Your Mind

Imagine, as you are reading a story, that the text says, "Cinderella looked beautiful, even in her clothes made of rags." At this point, I would stop reading and say, "That's a funny picture. I can see her pretty face and hair, but I cannot picture her looking pretty in ragged old clothing." Then I'd continue to read the story.

2. Predicting from the Text What Comes Next

At the opportune time, perhaps the moment that Cinderella's fairy godmother is introduced into the story, I'd stop reading and say, "I can predict what will happen now. I bet that the fairy godmother will get Cinderella a new dress. That's what I predict." Then I'd go back to reading the text. When I approach the episode that confirms my prediction, I would stop, put my finger to my forehead, and say, "My prediction was right. The fairy godmother got her a dress and everything else, too."

3. Asking Questions About the Text

When I believe that there might be several alternatives for the direction of the story's plot, I'd ask myself a question, out loud, just before the event occurs. As Cinderella dances with the prince I might say, "I wonder if Cinderella's clothes will turn back into rags at midnight?" Then I would proceed to read on to answer the question.

4. Rereading to Clarify Ideas

Often stories have ideas that are different from what was expected. The concept of a fairy godmother could be unexpected when the child hears the story for the first time. What this character represents might cause conceptual confusion. I've reread sections of stories, like the episode where the fairy godmother magically changes a mouse into a horse, and rags into a beautiful dress, that illustrate the concepts that might need clarification. Asking a question with my finger pointed to my temple ("I wonder why she's called fairy godmother and not just godmother?") and then rereading sections that illustrate the idea is a strategy that works to get children started. When I approach these "hazy" sections of the text, I answer my own questions by using text that seems best to justify the meaning. "She's a fairy godmother, because she just waves a magic wand and poof— she gets you something. I have a real godmother, but she doesn't have a magic wand. She gets me things with money in the store." That clarifies that idea.

5. Rereading for Word Meaning

One of the best ways to build vocabulary during reading is to predict word meaning from context. Demonstrating this with thinkalongs helps children understand that rereading is effective for learning words. When I approach a word whose meaning might be new for some, I stop. If, for example, the word "necromancer" were used instead of "magician," I would attempt to figure out the meaning by asking myself, "I wonder what this word means? It says that the fairy godmother is a necromancer. I am going to reread to try and find out what the word means." Reread and say, "Aha, I know what it means. It must mean that she is magical because she can make marvelous things happen." Then I'd continue to reread.

6. Personalizing the Text

Most stories include ideas that can be related to personal experiences. When I approach a section of a story that has personal meaning for me, I stop and think along. I might say, for example, "I remember when I wanted to go to a school dance. My mom said I could go after I cleaned my room. That's what Cinderella's stepmother said to her. After you clean, you can go."

It takes many demonstrations of thinkalongs for children to learn how to use this self-monitoring technique. But the repeated modeling does pay off when used for at least a month's time, biweekly.

Listening Strategies: Procedure 2

I have found that after several thinkalong story reading sessions, children begin to notice what you are doing. As you carry out the activity some may shout out, "I know what you are doing. You are talking about the story." I recommend that after several children tell you about your behavior, you direct the children to watch your actions. I say, "I want you to watch me as I think along. After I finish reading the story, we will make a list of all of the strategies that you see me use when I think about the story." After reading, I ask the children to tell what I did. I record responses, in children's words, on a large piece of easel paper or the chalkboard. Then we read these as a group.

Thinkalong Worksheets: Procedure 3

After working through procedure 2, I make a worksheet of the thinkalongs that the children suggested. I reproduce this for all of the children as soon after the session as possible. If you carry out a thinkalong story session in the morning, it is ideal to have the sheet by the afternoon, or the very next day at the latest. I begin the next thinkalong story-reading session in the usual manner, but this time, I provide each child with a crayon, marker, or pencil and the thinkalong monitoring sheet (**Figure 3-12**). I begin by saying, "I will think along as I read. This time, you check the thinkalong strategies that you see me use during reading." At the end of the reading, I ask, "Which thinkalongs did I use?" Asking children to notice your behavior tells them that modeling is teaching. I have found that children learn faster and more easily when they have the opportunity to see me do what I want them to do. Again, carry out this procedure several times, for repeating the activity helps children learn the strategy.

Working in Pairs to Think Along: Procedure 4

After children have had many experiences with thinkalongs and seem to understand the purposes of thinking along, they can begin to use the thinkalongs independently. I've grouped children into pairs. I've asked them to take turns, one reading and the other monitoring the thinkalongs used.

Thinking along takes a long time to learn. Children who use these strategies automatically will be able to tell what they see you doing

```
┌─────────────────────────────────────────────┐
│  THINKALONG MONITORING SHEET                │
├─────────────────────────────────────────────┤
│              Thinkalongs                     │
│                                              │
│                          CHECK HERE          │
│                                              │
│  Make a picture in my mind    _____    │
│                                              │
│  Predict from the text        _____    │
│                                              │
│  Ask myself questions         _____    │
│                                              │
│  Reread to clarify ideas      _____    │
│                                              │
│  Reread for word meaning      _____    │
│                                              │
│  Personalize the text         _____    │
│                                              │
│  My Name: _____    │
│                                              │
│  My Partner: _____    │
│                                              │
│  Date: _____            │
│                                              │
└─────────────────────────────────────────────┘
```

Figure 3-12

within several sessions. For children who have little knowledge of what they do when they read, however, it may take several months to master the strategy. Building this kind of awareness takes patience. I find that working with small groups, each using one thinkalong at a time, is ideal. I try to allow ample time for each of the children to read and think along independently and with another child. I also provide rehearsal time for children.

SELF-MONITORING SHEET—THINKALONGS

Thinkalong	Always	Some-times	Never
I know when I don't understand something.			
I ask myself questions to understand the story.			
I make a picture in my mind to help me understand the story.			
I reread to help myself understand.			
I personalize the ideas and relate them to my own experiences. I think about something I know that fits into the new information.			
I reread when I don't know what a word means.			
Sometimes I predict what will happen next in a story.			

Name: _____

Date: _____

Figure 3-13

Self-Monitoring Thinkalongs

I have adapted the self-monitoring checksheet (**Figure 3-13**) from one developed by Carol S. Brown (1991) and have found that when this activity is carried out weekly, for several months, many children begin to self-monitor their thought processes. I've modeled using this checksheet by reading the thinkalong statement printed on the left side of the sheet, first. Then I provide an example of the thinkalong. I might say, for example (after reading), "I know when I don't understand something"), "I can tell that I don't understand something when I can't tell the story in my own words." Self-monitoring thinkalong strategies, much like self-monitoring retelling, can be taught in an individual conference setting.

One final but important thought: *Thinking along breaks the natural flow of language and comprehension of the text. This activity, therefore, should be an addition to, and not a substitute for, reading stories to children without interruption or children reading themselves.*

JOURNAL ACTIVITIES

The following journal activities will help you reflect and learn more about reading comprehension and children's growth. Record and read your observations thinking about the strategies that were described in Chapter III. As you record observations and read them, you may gain insight into children's ways of comprehending what they read.

1. Read a story to a preschool-age child (two through four). After reading, carry out an unguided oral retelling. Then work through the same activity with an older child (six through nine). Tape and transcribe the retellings. Compare retellings. What do you notice?

2. Do a guided retelling with a preschooler and an older child. Compare the results. Respond to the results in a narrative format in your journal.

3. Use thinkalongs when you have a problem with your car, tax

return, job application form, or medical insurance claim form. Write your responses and reactions to using these in your daily life.

4. How might you be able to incorporate some of the ideas in this text to things you are already doing in your classroom? Write these ideas in your journal.

A FINAL WORD

We know that reading comprehension is a complex process. It involves language, perceptions, prior knowledge about the world, and prior knowledge about how language works. The ability to make meaning from texts of all sorts depends, in large part, on physical, emotional, social, and academic development as well. If you think about it, however, reading is really like many other human behaviors. The human mind responds best when things are familiar and comfortable. The human mind is probably the most amazing machine in this universe. It develops economical strategies to make meaning not only of written texts but of everything in life. The strategies suggested in this text are economical, can be used across all curriculum areas, and, for children of all ages. They are designed to guide children to become independent readers. I propose that the strategies discussed in this book are compatible with most problem-solving situations. This book offers you the chance to ask questions to help you assess your interactions with your students and how they affect the development of independent readers and writers. The following questions can serve as your own guide for observing and reflecting on teaching behaviors.

1. Do I read and share my ideas orally on a regular basis?

2. Do I provide time for independent reading for myself and the children?

3. Do I schedule activities so that there is always some time for sharing ideas about books?

4. Do I model strategies regularly so that I provide children with behaviors for helping them read independently?

5. Do I plan time so that I meet with children individually as well as in small groups?

6. Do I respond to children's spontaneous desires to share what they read and write?

7. Do I respect the individualities of each child?

8. Do I look at my behavior and try to understand how my actions affect children's learning?

BIBLIOGRAPHY

Arbuthnot, M. H., and Sutherland, Z. (1977). *Children and books* (5th ed.). Glenview, IL: Scott Foresman.

Beckman, D. (1972). Interior space: The things of education. *National Elementary Principal, 52,* 45–49.

Bird, M. (1980). Reading comprehension strategies: A direct teaching approach. *Dissertation Abstracts International, 41,* (6) 2506–A.

Bissett, D. (1969). The amount and effect of recreational reading in selected fifth grade classes. Doctoral dissertation, Syracuse University.

Brown, C. S. (1984). A tutorial procedure for enhancing the reading comprehension of college students. Doctoral Dissertation, University of Pennsylvania. *Dissertation Abstracts International, 47,* 3719–A.

Brown, C. S. (1991, May). *Using portfolios to monitor comprehension processes.* Paper presented at the Rider College Reading Language Arts Conference, Lawrenceville, NJ.

Brown, C. S., and Lytle, S. L. (1988). Merging assessment and instruction: Protocols in the classroom. In S. M. Glazer, L. W. Searfoss, & L. M. Gentile (Eds.), *Reexamining reading diagnosis: New trends and procedures.* (pp. 94–102). Newark, DE: International Reading Association.

Brown, H., and Cambourne, B. (1987). *Read and retell.* Portsmouth, NH: Heinemann.

Corcoran, V. (1991). *Qualitative study of children's perceptions of reading behavior and their ability to comprehend* (Research study). Lawrenceville, NJ: Rider College.

Cullinan, B. E. (1989). *Literature and the child (2nd ed.).* NY: Harcourt, Brace, Jovanovich, Inc.

Dale, P. S. (1976). *Language development: Structure and function* (2nd ed.). Seattle, WA: Holt, Rinehart and Winston.

Eddy, B. L., and Gould, K. A. (1990). "Comprehension system 8": A teacher's perspective. *Literacy: Issues and Practices, 7,* 70–75.

Farr, R. (1990, May). *Thinkalong strategies.* Paper presented at the meeting of the International Reading Association, Atlanta, Georgia.

Glazer, S. M. (1991). Behaviors reflecting emotional involvements during reading and writing activities. *Reading, Writing, and Learning Disabilities International, 7,* 219–230.

Glazer, S. M., and Searfoss, L. W. (1988). *Reading diagnosis and instruction: A C-A-L-M approach.* Englewood Cliffs, NJ: Prentice Hall.

Goodman, K. (1986). *What's whole in whole language?* NY: Scholastic.

Gordon, C. (1990). Changes in readers' and writers' metacognitive knowledge: Some observations. *Reading Research and Instruction, 30,* 1–14.

Holdaway, D. (1986). The structure of natural learning as a basis for literacy instruction. In M. R. Sampson (ed.), *The pursuit of literacy* (pp. 56–72). Dubuque, IA.

Lindfors, J. W. (1987). *Children's language and learning* (2nd ed.). Englewood Cliffs, NJ: Prentice Hall.

Lipson, M. Y. (1982). Learning new information from text: The role of prior knowledge and reading ability. *Journal of reading behavior, 14,* 243–261.

Morrow, L. M., (1985). *Promoting voluntary reading in school and home.* Bloomington, IN: Phi Delta Kappa Educational Foundation.

Morrow, L. M. and Weinstein, C. S. (1986). Encouraging voluntary reading: The impact of a literature program on children's use of library centers. *Reading Research Quarterly, 21,* 330–346.

Palincsar, A. S., and Brown, A. L. (1984). Reciprocal teaching of comprehension fostering and comprehension monitoring activities. In *Cognition and Instruction, 1,* 117–175.

Reed, A. J. S. (1988). *Comics to classics: A parent's guide to books for teens and preteens.* Newark, DE: International Reading Association.

Routman, R. (1991). *Invitations: Changing as teachers and learners K–12.* Portsmouth, NH: Heinemann.

Russavage, P. M., and Arick, K. L. (1988). Thinkalong: A strategic approach to improving comprehension. *Reading: Issues and Practices, 5,* 32–41.

Searfoss, L. W., and Readence, J. E. (1989). *Helping children learn to read* (2nd ed.). Englewood Cliffs, NJ: Prentice Hall.

Smith, F. (1985). *Reading without nonsense* (2nd ed.). NY: Teachers College Press.

Sullivan, J. (1978). Comparing strategies of good and poor comprehenders. *Journal of Reading, 21,* 710–715.

Wilson, R. and Russavage, P. (1989). Schoolwide application of comprehension strategies. In J. D. Coley and S. S. Clewell (Eds.), *Reading issues and practices* (pp. 45–46). Maryland: State of Maryland Reading Association.

Winograd, P. And Greenlee, M. (1986). Students need a balanced reading program. *Educational Leadership, 43,* 16–21.

LITERATURE MENTIONED IN THE TEXT

Anonymous. *Go Ask Alice.* Prentice-Hall, 1971.

Avi. *The Fighting Ground.* Lippincott, 1985.

Brown, M. (Illustrator). *Cinderella.* Scribner's, 1954.

Carle, E. *The Very Hungry Caterpillar.* Philomel Books, 1970.

Cleary, B. *Ramona and Her Father.* Morrow, 1977.

Clements, A. *Big Al.* Picture Book Studio, 1988.

Freeman, D. *Dandelion.* Viking, 1964.

Gaines, E. *The Autobiography of Miss Jane Pitman.* Doubleday, 1971.

Galdone, P. *The House That Jack Built.* McGraw-Hill, 1961.

Giff, P. R. *Today Was a Terrible Day.* Viking, 1980.

Greenberg, J. *The Pig-Out Blues.* Farrar, Straus & Giroux, 1982.

Greenwald, S. *All the Way to Wits' End.* Little Brown, 1979.

Greenwald, S. *Valentine Rosy.* Dell, 1984.

Hamilton, V. *The Magical Adventures of Pretty Pearl.* Harper & Row, 1983.

Hill, E. *Where's Spot?* Putnam, 1984.

Janeczko, P. *Bridges to Cross.* Macmillan, 1986.

Kerr, M. E. *Dinky Hocker Shoots Smack.* Harper & Row, 1972.

Kuskin, C. *Just Like Everyone Else.* Harper & Row, 1959.

Leaf, M. *Ferdinand.* Viking, 1936.

Le Cain, E. (Illustrator). *Cinderella.* Bradbury, 1972.

L'Engle, M. *Dragons in the Water.* Farrar, Straus & Giroux, 1980.

Lewis, C. S. *The Lion, the Witch, and the Wardrobe.* Macmillan, 1986.

Mazer, N. F. *When We First Met.* Macmillan, 1982.

Miller, F. *The Truth Trap.* Dutton, 1980.

Myers, W. D. *Hoops.* Dell, 1981.

Ness, E. *Sam, Bangs and Moonshine.* Holt, Rinehart & Winston, 1966.

Newton, S. *I Will Call It Georgie's Blues.* Viking, 1983.

Oechsli, K. *Mice at Bat.* Harper & Row, 1986.

Packard, E. *Deadwood City* (Choose Your Own Adventure). Bantam, 1980.

Peck, R. N. *A Day No Pigs Would Die.* Knopf, 1972.

Potter, B. *The Tale of Peter Rabbit.* Warne, 1902.

Sharmat, M. *Gregory the Terrible Eater.* Scholastic, 1980.

Sharmat, M. W. *Mooch the Messy.* Harper & Row, 1976.

Strasser, T. *Friends Till the End.* Delacorte, 1981.

Twain, M. *The Adventures of Huckleberry Finn.* Scholastic, 1983.

Voigt, C. *Homecoming.* Macmillan, 1981.

White, E. B. *Charlotte's Web.* Harper & Row, 1952.

APPENDIX

Children's Literature That Facilitates Comprehension

Literature that helps children read and understand guides the development of comprehension. Several characteristics mentioned in this book help children to read easily. These include:

- Easy-to-read books, with predictable plots and language, in which pictures match words and help tell the story;
- Books with definitive story structure;
- Books that lend themselves to prediction before reading;
- Books that help children use thinkalongs.

The following book list can serve as a guide for developing a classroom library. The list is coded for age groups:

     PS = preschool, ages 2–4
      E = elementary, ages 5–7
     UE = upper elementary, ages 8–9
     PT = preteen, ages 10–12

Aliki. *Go Tell Aunt Rhody.* Illus. by author. Macmillan, 1974.
   This song-turned-into-story book has repeated sentence patterns that guide children to predict what comes next. (PS, E)

Barrett, J. *Animals Should Definitely Not Wear Clothing.* Atheneum, 1970.
   This book about putting animals in clothing is fun and lends itself to both predictable outcomes and language patterns. (E, UE)

Briggs, R. *Snowman.* Illus. by author. Random House, 1978.
   This intricate picture book without words permits children with limited reading vocabulary to read a story. The story structure is well-developed, includes all story elements, and provides children with extensive illustrations from which to create a simply or intricately told story. (PS, E, UE)

Brown, M. *Stone Soup.* Scribner's, 1947.
   Selfish motives turn to sharing when a wise one pulls a community together by making soup from stones, or that's how it begins. This is perfect for thinking along and developing prediction during reading, making pictures in one's mind, and asking questions during reading. (E, UE)

Cohen, B. *Roses.* Lothrop, Lee & Shepard, 1984.
   This modern version of the Beauty and the Beast involves Courtney and the frightened owner of a flower shop. Love and romance will entice the reader into this well-planned story. (UE, PT)

Cormier, R. *Eight Plus One.* Bantam, 1980.
   This is a book of short stories, each preceded by an introduction by the author, which explains his thoughts about how and why the story was created. This book is wonderful for guiding the young writer into creating stories. (UE, PT)

Eastman, P. *Are You My Mother?* Random House, 1960.
This easy-to-read book with repeated language, simple plot, and illustrations that match the words on the page is appropriate for all comprehension activities, including recognizing story structure and thinkalongs before and during reading. (PS, E)

Galdone, P. *Henny Penny.* Illus. by author. Houghton Mifflin, 1968.
Predictable language, pictures that match the language, and definitive story structure make this book a must. (PS, E)

Johnson, C. *Harold and the Purple Crayon.* Harper & Row, 1955.
The definitive story structure helps children see all elements of story clearly. (PS, E)

Lowry, L. *Find a Stranger, Say Good-Bye.* Houghton Mifflin, 1978.
This book about Natalie, an adopted daughter attempting to locate her biological parents, propels the reader into a well-constructed story. It lends itself to thinkalongs, as well as understanding story structure. (UE, PT)

Lobel, A. *The Random House Book of Mother Goose.* Random House, 1986.
All libraries must include traditional literature. Mother Goose rhymes and stories delight the heart and help youngsters predict language and story as well. (PS, E, UE, PT)

Martin, Jr., B. *Polar Bear, Polar Bear, What Do You Hear?* Illus. by Eric Carle. Henry Holt, 1991.
Repeated language, wonderful illustrations that match the language, rhythm, and rhyme are a winning combination. (PS, E)

Mazer, H. *Cave Under the City.* Crowell, 1986.
This is a story about Tolley and how the Great Depression results in his need to assume responsibility for his five-year-old brother. This historically based novel lends itself to the development of story structure. (UE, PT)

Novak, M. *Mr. Floop's Lunch.* New York: Orchard, 1990.
Definitive story structure, the theme of sharing, and predictable language make this book perfect for guiding all aspects of comprehension. (PS, E)

Peck, R. *Blossom Culp and the Sleep of Death.* Delacorte, 1986.
This science fiction story concerns Blossom, who is haunted by an ancient Egyptian princess. With the help of her friend, Blossom takes the princess back to her place in history. This is part of a series of Blossom stories with definitive story structure and enticing plots. (UE, PT)

Pinkwater, D. *The Sharkout Boys and the Avocado of Death.* Lothrop, Lee & Shepard, 1982.
This humorous novel includes a series of zany episodes that provide adventure as well as developing story structure and a desire to read. (UE, PT)

Seuss, Dr. *The Cat in the Hat.* Random House, 1957.
This and other books written by Dr. Seuss include predictable language, words and pictures that match, and well-developed episodic structure. (PS, E, UE)

Stern, P. *I Was a Fifteen-Year-Old Blimp.* Harper & Row, 1985.
This novel concerns a young girl's desperate desire to be thin and attractive to boys. Her driving need results in a dangerous attempt to lose weight quickly. This text vividly illustrates a story's problem and resolution. (UE, PT)

Viorst, J. *Alexander and the Terrible, Horrible, No Good, Very Bad Day.* Atheneum, 1976.
This story about a bad day when nothing goes right has definitive story structure, predictable language, and a plot that makes it a must for every classroom library. (E, UE, PT)

Wayne, K. P. *Max, the Dog That Refused To Die.* Alpine, 1979.
This heartwarming true story about Max, a seriously injured Doberman pinscher who has been separated from his family in Yosemite, supplies children with a well-written text and is difficult to put down. (UE, PT)

Wood, A. *The Napping House.* Harcourt Brace Jovanovich, 1984.
Cumulative language patterns where each previous line is repeated as the story progresses help youngsters predict the language and plot. (PT, E, UE)